ABORIGINAL PEOPLES OF CANADA

MÉTIS

Jennifer Howse

Weigl

Published by Weigl Educational Publishers Limited
6325 10th Street S.E.
Calgary, Alberta, Canada T2H 2Z9

Website: www.weigl.com
Copyright ©2011 Weigl Educational Publishers Limited

Library and Archives Canada Cataloguing in Publication
Howse, Jennifer
          Métis / author: Jennifer Howse ; editor: Heather Kissock.
(Aboriginal peoples of Canada)
Includes index.
Also available in electronic format.
ISBN 978-1-55388-644-0 (bound).--ISBN 978-1-55388-650-1 (pbk.)
          1. Métis--Juvenile literature. I. Kissock, Heather II. Title.
III. Series: Aboriginal peoples of Canada (Calgary, Alta.)
E99.M47H697 2010   j971.004'97   C2009-907316-1

Printed in the United States of America in North Mankato, Minnesota
1 2 3 4 5 6 7 8 9 14 13 12 11 10

062010
WEP230610

Photograph and Text Credits
Cover: Manitoba Museum; Alamy: pages 5, 7, 11L, 12T, 12B, 15; Canadian Museum of Civilization: page 9B (III-DD-82 a-b, D2003-15433); Corbis: page 10M; Courtesy of Verne Equinox: page 14; Getty Images: pages 4, 10L, 10R, 11M, 11R, 13; Glenbow Museum: pages 9M (AR-29), 20 (AR-281); Government of the Northwest Territories: pages 21, 23; Courtesy of Fred Lang: pages 8, 16, 17; Manitoba Museum: page 9T; Mary Evans Picture Library: page 6.

Every reasonable effort has been made to trace ownership and to obtain permission to reprint copyright material. The publishers would be pleased to have any errors or omissions brought to their attention so that they may be corrected in subsequent printings.

All of the Internet URLs given in this book were valid at the time of publication. However, due to the dynamic nature of the Internet, some addresses may have changed, or sites may have ceased to exist since publication. While the author and publisher regret any inconvenience this may cause readers, no responsibility for any such changes can be accepted by either the author or the publisher.

We gratefully acknowledge the financial support of the Government of Canada through the Canada Book Fund for our publishing activities.

PROJECT COORDINATOR Heather Kissock

DESIGN Terry Paulhus

ILLUSTRATOR Martha Jablonski-Jones

Contents

The People

The Métis are one of Canada's **Aboriginal Peoples**. The name *Métis* is a French term meaning "mixed." The Métis were named this because of their unique **ancestry**.

More than 400 years ago, European men travelled to the land now called Canada to work in the **fur trade**. Here, they started families with **First Nations** women. The children of these European men and First Nations women were called Métis. Today, the name Métis is used by people who have both First Nations and European ancestors.

NET LINK

To read more about the history of the Métis, go to **www.metisnation.org/culture/home.html**.

Métis Homes

LOG HOUSES

In the past, the Métis lived in houses made from logs and **sod**. The logs were cut to fit together like a puzzle. Then, the logs were stacked on top of each other. Gaps in the log walls were filled with a mixture of mud and grass. Windows did not have glass. Deer hides were used instead. The hides were stretched and scraped thin enough for sunlight to shine through.

Métis Ideas

The inside of the log house had rafters, which are poles that run across the ceiling. The Métis stored their food in cloth slings that hung over the rafters.

Métis families were away from their homes many times during the year. They travelled to hunt and to take goods to **trading posts**. When travelling, the Métis slept in teepees.

Métis Clothing

JACKETS

The Métis often wore jackets made from deerskin or moosehide. Sometimes, blankets were used to make coats called capotes.

PANTS, LEGGINGS, SKIRTS, AND SHIRTS

Métis men wore pants and shirts. Women wore shirts and skirts. When the weather grew cold, the women would wear leggings under their skirts. Animal hides, wool, cotton, and velvet were all used to make these clothes.

HATS

Some Métis hats were made from animal skins or fur. Others were made of European materials, such as felt. Most hats were decorated with fancy beadwork.

MÉTIS SASH

Métis men wore a sash around their waist. The sash was woven from red, yellow, green, and blue wools.

MOCCASINS AND STOCKINGS

Moosehide was used to make moccasins for the Métis to wear on their feet. Woollen stockings were worn under the moccasins.

Hunting and Gathering

BISON

Bison was the main food source for Métis living on the Prairies. Bison meat was mixed with fat and berries to make food called pemmican.

BANNOCK

The Métis blended bison grease with flour to make bannock. This bread was served with meat and vegetables.

BERRIES

The Métis picked berries from bushes that grew locally. Blueberries were one type of berry that could be used to make pemmican.

The Métis relied on the land for much of their food. They hunted game and fished in local waters. In the summer months, they grew vegetable gardens. When Europeans arrived in the area, the Métis traded extra meat and hides for flour and sugar.

FISH Fish were a major food source for the Métis. They caught and ate fish such as salmon, pickerel, and trout. Fish were often used in soups.

DEER As well as a source of clothing, deer were used for food. Deer meat, or venison, was put in stews or cooked and eaten on its own.

TEA Tea was an important beverage for the Métis. They boiled the leaves of flowers, herbs, and trees to make tea.

Métis Tools

BISON

Long ago, the Métis used bison parts to make tools. Bones were used to make knives, arrowheads, and shovels. Bison skin was stretched and shaped into buckets, ropes, and bags. The animal's horns became spoons and ladles.

COOKING

The Métis cooked food using containers made from bison hide and willow branches. They also used pots and pans made from cast iron and other metals.
These cooking tools were brought from Europe.

NET LINK

Other Métis tools are described at **www.albertasource.ca/METIS/eng/ culture_lifeways/arts_crafts_tools.htm**.

Moving from Place to Place

CANOE

The Métis often travelled by water to take goods to trading posts. They used York boats to carry big shipments. A York boat had a flat bottom. Oars were used to steer the boat up or down the river.

When the Métis had to cross a river, they removed the wheels of the Red River cart and used the cart as a raft.

Red River carts were another way to take items to and from trading posts. These carts were pulled by horses or oxen.

Métis Music and Dance

Like their French and Scottish ancestors, the Métis made music using fiddles. The fiddles were usually accompanied by the tapping of heels, spoons, or tin pans.

When fiddle music is playing, Métis dancers often perform a dance called a jig. Jigs are very fast dances. The dancers use their shoes to pound out **rhythms** in time with the music.

NET LINK

To watch a Métis jig being performed, surf to **www.youtube.com/watch?v=mZsqCGstJdQ**.

How the Moon Came to Be

Long ago, the Sun was the only object to light the sky. There was no moon. A man called the Caretaker of the Sun made sure it shone brightly by burning a great fire all day long.

The man had been taking care of the Sun for many years, but he was getting old. One day, the man called his two children to him. He sat down with them and made them promise to keep the fire burning. He told them that, if the fire did not burn, all of the people and animals on Earth would die. Shortly after their talk, the father left his children forever.

It was now the children's job to start the Sun's fire. However, when morning came the next day, the children began arguing over who should do the job.

The people on Earth began to worry when the Sun did not appear. They sent a Wisakecahk to the Sun to see what was happening. When he arrived, the children were still fighting. Wisakecahk became angry. He separated the children and gave each of them the job of keeping a fire burning. The boy was to keep the Sun's fire burning in the day. The girl was to keep a different fire burning at night. This was how the Moon came to be.

Métis Art

The Métis decorated most of their clothing with porcupine quills or glass beads. The beading was very colourful and detailed. Common designs included flowers and vines.

Some clothes also had designs embroidered onto them. Métis women would gather dyed moose or caribou hairs into bunches and sew them onto clothes in different patterns. This type of sewing was called tufting.

NET LINK

Read more about Métis embroidery and beading at **www.metisnation.org/ gov_bodies/mnoyc/MOHM/Beading.htm**.

Métis Tufting

Materials
Construction paper
White pencil crayon
Cotton balls
Dry paint
Glue

Directions
1. Take a black piece of construction paper and a white pencil crayon. Use the pencil to make dots and create shapes of flowers, stems, and leaves.
2. Put the dry paint in small separate bowls.
3. Dip the cotton balls into the dry paint until they are covered with colour.
4. Glue the cotton balls inside the pattern you drew on the paper.
5. A colourful picture will slowly be revealed as each of the cotton balls are glued into place.

Glossary

Aboriginal Peoples: original inhabitants of an area

ancestry: relating to relatives who lived a long time ago

First Nations: members of Canada's Aboriginal community who are not Inuit or Métis

fur trade: the exchange of furs for European goods

rhythms: musical beats

sod: soil that has grass growing in it

trading posts: places where people went to trade furs for other items

tuned: adjusted the sound

Index